High School Testing

Knowledge That Saves Money

Lee Binz,
The HomeScholar

First Printing, 2013

Printed in the United States of America
Cover Design by Robin Montoya
Edited by Kimberly Charron

ISBN: 1535545712
ISBN-13: 978-1535545716

High School Testing

Knowledge That Saves Money

What are Coffee Break Books?

High School Testing is part of The HomeScholar's Coffee Break Book series.

Designed especially for parents who don't want to spend hours and hours reading a 400-page book on homeschooling high school, each book combines Lee's practical and friendly approach with detailed, but easy-to-digest information, perfect to read over a cup of coffee at your favorite coffee shop!

Never overwhelming, always accessible and manageable, each book in the series will give parents the tools they need to tackle the tasks of homeschooling high school, one warm sip at a time.

Everything about these Coffee Break Books is designed to suggest simplicity, ease and comfort - from the size (fits in a purse), to the font and paragraph length (easy on the eyes), to the price (the same as a Starbucks Venti Triple Caramel Macchiato). Unlike a fancy coffee drink, however, these books are guilt-free pleasures you will want to enjoy again and again!

Table of Contents

Introduction

The Joy of Tests

Although I have never been a big proponent of standardized tests, they can be useful for many homeschoolers. High school tests can serve as an inexpensive method of satisfying annual testing requirements in your state, and some can help your high school student earn college credit. For those who are college bound, standardized tests (such as the ACT and SAT) are requirements for admission. Learning about the different tests can help you use them as tools, instead of letting them be tyrants, so it's worth considering whether your student should take one. Here are some of the ways standardized tests can help your child thrive.

Measure Student Ability

I can't tell you how many times a parent has told me, "My child isn't doing very well," only to find out (after taking a standardized test) that they are above grade level. As I was consoling one mother, I encouraged her to look at her children's annual assessments, to see if her concerns were truly valid.

"Holy cow!" she said. "I just got the results back from the CAT the boys took recently. Christopher's overall score was 99%. This included vocabulary, comprehension, spelling, language mechanics, language expression, mathematics computation, math concepts, study skills, science, and social studies. Matthew scored 96% overall on the above subjects as well. Ok, so I can relax a little on this homeschooling thing."

Assess Relative Strength

One drawback of homeschooling is that we become so close to our children that we can easily identify their weaknesses.

Unfortunately, while it may be easy for us to see their failures, we lose sight of where they are in the grand scheme of things, and how they compare to others. We know their weaknesses. But does that mean they are below grade level?

Learning at their Level

Using a test can help you identify what level test book your child should use in each subject. Why bother teaching something a child already knows? It is a waste of time. Instead, assess where they are and then begin teaching at the point they will learn something new. For math, you can use an online placement test and then an end-of-chapter test in the textbook to see what they already know.

Assess High School Credits

Some tests can be used to determine if your child has achieved high school credit. SAT Subject Tests in such subjects as French or American History can prove that a child of any age has achieved a high school amount of learning in the subject. Standardized tests can tell you if your child is ready for a challenge, or if it's best to wait until later before starting on the next level.

Meet College Admission Requirements

Colleges almost always require test scores for admission. Whether students choose the SAT or ACT is less important. Colleges want to see a standardized test score in order to help determine college readiness. Practicing fill-in-the-bubble tests for the SAT can provide practice for college admission tests. As students become familiar with bubble tests and crowded testing environments, they are also practicing key skills needed for college admission tests. Taking the SAT or ACT is often the first time homeschoolers are in a group-testing environment.

Practice for College Tests

When I speak to colleges about homeschoolers, they are almost universally positive and happy about their level of preparation. But one college representative did have a concern. He had seen some students who were so used to natural learning that they weren't prepared for bubble tests. He felt this represented a homeschool weakness. While I disagree that it is a common problem, it's certainly worth mentioning.

Tests are usually required in college. High school tests can help children prepare for the kinds of tests colleges give. This doesn't mean you have to test all the time, of course, only enough to be prepared!

Save Money on College Costs

Certain tests can help you save money on the cost of college. Scholarships are often tied to SAT or ACT scores, so practicing and planning for these tests can provide scholarship money. Some parents use testing to document college level learning by using AP and CLEP tests. These tests can result in college credit, and may reduce the number of years you pay for college.

Outside Documentation of Grades

Reflect and document your homeschool grades with outside documentation of learning. Without using tests at every juncture, a single subject test can provide some proof of learning from an impartial third party, such as the College Board. Whether documentation comes from a college admission test, subject test, or community college course grade, these tests can prove the student has the underlying knowledge necessary to succeed.

Practice for Life

Bubble tests do exist in daily life as well. Voting is often done as a bubble test of sorts, and the test to obtain a driver's license requires filling in the bubbles. You may write tests on the job, from feedback forms to personality profiles, and your child needs to feel comfortable with the process of testing.

Emergency Preparedness

Testing can help you plan for a potential homeschool emergency in the future. A yearly test can provide a record of what your children know, at least as a rough estimate. This is important during a family crisis, even if school was hit-or-miss for a while due to illness or trauma.

I have recommended using standardized test scores to many parents to calm their fears after a year of crisis. "Look!" I say. "You have *not* failed your children! Their test scores have improved or stayed the same!"

Determining Grades

Tests can be used as a tool for determining grades. They are only one weapon, not the whole army, so don't use them as the *sole* source of grades. Still, you can use any assessment for calculating grades. The SAT measures math and you can use it as a portion of your child's math grade. The IOWA test measures vocabulary, so you can use it as a portion of your child's English grade.

Avoid Anxiety

Any new experience can cause anxiety. When a test is a new experience, it can cause fear. By providing the occasional test, children can learn through experience that nothing bad will happen, there are always distractions, and their best is good enough. The PSAT can provide practice for the SAT, so children don't panic when taking it. It gives kids practice taking tests around a large number of strangers with strange smells and often even stranger looks.

Determine Course Titles

It can be difficult to come up with appropriate course titles. One of the easiest ways is to steal titles from subject tests. If your child takes a subject test called "Microeconomics" and you are stuck trying to decide what to call the class, simply use the name of the test.

Motivate Competitors

I have two competitive boys and *everything* was a competition in our home. I was always careful to give the boys the same number of presents at Christmas. I remember the first time they caught on to this. I found them weighing presents with a bathroom scale to see who had the most by the pound. These boys were *born* competitive!

Naturally, when it came to end-of-chapter and college admission tests, both my children wanted the high score. With both of them motivated to get the highest score, they studied, prepared, and laughed together. Tests can motivate competitive children, even if they are competitive and motivated within themselves rather than with their siblings.

Relax

Standardized tests are required by some states, and obeying your state homeschool law can help you *and* your child relax. Some employers and colleges want to see that you have followed your state regulations. Law enforcement and military recruiters may check up on you. It's good to know you have your bases covered. Even if you aren't going to interact with these agencies, it's nice to know you have a back-up plan in case anyone ever asks for proof that your homeschool educated your children.

The Joy of Tests

It's ironic that I'm writing about the joy of tests! I have entire speeches, book chapters, and webinars on how to avoid testing in your homeschool! I'm not much of a grader and didn't make much use of quizzes, tests, and worksheets in our homeschool. Even so, I can see that the occasional standardized test can help homeschool parents (perhaps it's my Pollyanna nature, always looking at the bright side). Sure, tests can be annoying, and they definitely have their drawbacks, but I prefer to look on the bright side because there are so many benefits to standardized tests!

Chapter 1

Study for the SAT

Studying for a college entrance exam is worthwhile for most college-bound high school students. It's not a waste of time! Research has shown that preparation can increase SAT scores by 100 points. Better SAT scores can increase your child's chances of earning college admission and academic scholarships. Making test preparation a regular part of your high school experience will make it much easier for your student to succeed. Public school students may have trouble finding time to prepare for the test, but it can be a part of your homeschooler's total educational experience.

Like many homeschool parents, I understood that studying for the SAT test was necessary for college admission and financial aid, but was frustrated that I had to "teach to the test." My teenagers were also resistant. But the tests measure basic skills and of all the things I wanted my children to learn, reading, writing, and math were high on the priority list. Now that we are on the other side, we can all see the benefits of preparation!

- High scores helped my children earn great scholarships.
- They learned important essay writing skills.
- They mastered math concepts from basic to advanced.
- They gained confidence in their test-taking abilities.

The Basics

The SAT is a standardized college entrance exam with two sections that measure evidence-based reading and writing, and math skills. Each section is graded on a 200-800 scale. For each section, a grade of 500 is average, 600 is good, 700 is great, and 800 is perfect. Because there are two sections, a perfect score on the SAT is 1600. Prior to the newly designed SAT, a perfect score was 2400 because there were three sections. The test takes three hours, plus 50 minutes for the optional essay section, and is given at local high schools and some colleges. For more information, go to www.collegeboard.com.

Refreshing math skills can be helpful for a struggling student who might benefit from a regular review of concepts. Math review will also help an advanced student, who may not have gone over beginning concepts for many years. The reading section includes vocabulary students need to know in order to succeed in college. Instead of buying a vocabulary curriculum, you can use SAT preparation for your homeschool vocabulary studies.

I have to confess that the essay is my favorite part of the test. Essay writing is crucial to success in college. My youngest son thanked me for teaching him how to write a typical test essay.

Tools to Prepare

Before high school begins, you can prepare for the SAT by providing a quality education that includes reading, writing, and arithmetic. Penmanship is important as well, since part of the SAT is an optional hand-written essay seen by colleges. Homeschooling parents have the advantage on the SAT test when they provide a quality, well-rounded education for their child.

But how does a high school student prepare for such a test? There are some great test prep books, but I prefer the ones from The Princeton Review. I feel they have a youthful, conversational style that appeals to teenagers more than the dry, "business only" approach of other books. I used the book, *Cracking the SAT* by The Princeton Review. It has a short, easy to understand explanation of the test, and includes four complete exams. All the answers provide clear explanations.

In our homeschool, we completed one section of one practice test at a time. Each section is 25 minutes long. We used a timer to simulate a real testing environment. After completing a section, my children corrected their tests by themselves, and looked over the explanation of each wrong answer.

If they still had questions, my husband went over the explanation with them. For more practice, check out *500+ Practice Questions for the New SAT* by The Princeton Review. It has a section on what to expect in the new SAT along with *many* practice questions. The focus of this book is *only* sample questions. It gives clear, concise answers and explanations for every problem.

For students who need more essay writing practice, check out the AP English Language and Composition free response questions; the prompts make perfect practice for the SAT essay section. You can find sample free response questions on the College Board's AP English Language and Composition page. In fact, the AP

English Language and Composition exam makes a great ACT/SAT prep course when taken in junior year.

For more SAT math, reading, writing, and essay practice, you can also visit the Khan Academy website at khanacademy.org/sat. In cooperation with the College Board, Khan Academy offers free information, practice tests, quizzes, video lessons, and hints.

Other kinds of test preparation can also increase scores and yield great dividends. Some students learn better without textbooks. For the reading and writing section, you can prepare your child using a "real books" approach. Reading quality literature is the best preparation.

Many test preparation companies offer classic literature that highlights SAT vocabulary words. Kaplan publishes a series of books called SAT Score-Raising Classics. They are books such as *Frankenstein*, *Wuthering Heights*, and *The Scarlet Letter* with the text on one side of the page and vocabulary words in bold print. On the other side of the page, each word in bold is defined in simple terms. We used these books as a part of our regular curriculum choices, and they doubled as SAT preparation. I read aloud and my children read the vocabulary definitions over my shoulder as we went along.

Auditory learners might prefer the Verbal Advantage program for vocabulary development, with its audio CDs and CD-ROM guidebooks. There are also SAT prep video tutorials available through Standard Deviants (www.standarddeviants.com) and The Teaching Company that can provide vocabulary and math review for visual learners.

Practice Might Make Perfect

You can enroll your child in a formal SAT class at home, using a variety of online courses through test preparation companies such as the College Board, Kaplan, or The Princeton Review. This may be a good option for a student who is a visual or auditory learner, or a student willing to do anything as long as it's on the computer. Your child can also take classes through a co-op (usually inexpensive) or a private course (usually pricey).

Our local library offered a practice test twice a year, through The Princeton Review. It was the most realistic practice we found, because it was a real test in a real test situation, graded so we had an objective score for each child. The SAT is such a *long* test that we were thankful our kids could try it in a safe environment before they took it for real.

Studying for the SAT can benefit your homeschool, but it's possible to go overboard. Studying for hours a day, for weeks on end may cause burnout. The last thing you want is to frustrate your teenager so much that they hate homeschooling. You want them to learn test-taking skills and reinforce basic skills, but do it with a light touch. Know your student, and trust your own judgment.

Accommodations for Homeschoolers

If your child struggles with learning challenges, it may be helpful to get an official diagnosis, and then pursue accommodation on the SAT. Accommodation requires a recent diagnosis from a doctor, and there are specific rules that must be followed.

If the essay is a stumbling block, you can also opt for the SAT or ACT test without the optional essay. The SAT or ACT work equally well for college admission. If you decide to avoid the essay, you can instead have your child take plenty of time on the college application essay, perhaps even explaining their difficulty with writing.

Look over the Dragon Naturally Speaking software to see if it can be a solution to help your child write college application essays and in other areas of school. Check the College Board Services for Students with Disabilities for more on accommodations.

Chapter 2

PSAT

Like the SAT, the PSAT is a college admission test overseen by the College Board. It meets most state homeschool testing requirements and covers reading, writing, and math, but doesn't include an essay. The PSAT is an inexpensive test compared to most annual assessments. In addition to being practice for the SAT, the PSAT can help you find a college, indicate career options your student might not have considered, and can lead to scholarships.

The complete name for the test is PSAT/NMSQT, which stands for Preliminary SAT/National Merit Scholarship Qualifying Test. The name can help you decipher the two functions of the PSAT. The first part, PSAT, means it's a practice test your child can take "for fun" to learn about the SAT. The second part, NMSQT, stands for National Merit Scholarship Qualifying Test, which means your child can take the test "for profit" as a junior. Either way can benefit your student.

Taking the PSAT "for Fun"!

The name PSAT means the test is preliminary, practice, or pre-SAT. Your child can take the test for practice in tenth or eleventh grade. I call this taking the test "for fun" because scores don't matter. The results are only for you, with no negative repercussions at all. You can use it as a starting point, before your child studies for the SAT and provide firsthand practice for the SAT. It is also used to estimate your child's SAT scores.

The PSAT measures math and evidence-based reading and writing. Each section is given a score of 160 to 760, with a total possible score between 320 and 1520 (prior to 2015, there were three sections with each scoring 20-80). Math makes up half the total score, and reading and writing make up the other half. The results are a good predictor of your child's future score on the SAT, even though the total possible score is lower than for the SAT. Knowing what score range your child is likely to attain on the SAT can help you find a college that will match your child's academic rigor.

The PSAT also provides practice taking standardized tests in a rotten environment. In a sea of contagious diseases, surrounded by tattoos, body piercings, and smelly teenagers, my sons sat in alphabetical order in a public school cafeteria. Certainly not a perfect situation for a test, but it was definitely good to see the setting of the SAT before the test score counted! Taking a timed test around strangers is difficult. It's more difficult when you haven't practiced first. The PSAT can provide practice taking a test in less than perfect, non-homeschooling conditions.

Comparative Function

Taking the test for fun will give you a percentile score, which compares your student against other bright, college-bound students of the same age. One of the few drawbacks of homeschooling is that you can lack a sense of where your child fits in the norm. You know perfectly well your student's foibles and weak areas, but often don't realize exactly how smart they are compared to the rest of the gene pool. This test can be a startling reminder of how efficient and effective homeschooling can be! Even struggling learners in a homeschool environment will often test average or above in standardized tests that compare them to other high school students.

The comparative function will also give you a helpful "data point" for your student if they simply do not test well. Nobody is perfect and there are students who won't test well, even though they are quite bright. Taking the PSAT for fun, without the risk of negative repercussions, can help you determine whether to use standardized test scores at all when applying to college. If your student does very poorly on the test, you can decide to use other methods to document your homeschool achievement.

Based on the "for fun" score, you can submit a portfolio instead of a test score. You might also decide to enroll your child in community college courses to prove college readiness. More options will be available when you have this information.

The test is good for comparison because it's standardized, which means that states requiring a test from homeschoolers will often accept the PSAT. Better still, it is an inexpensive test, so you can save money by using it. As far as tests go, the PSAT is a cheap way to meet your state's requirement for annual testing. In Washington state, for example, it's the best value for testing in tenth and eleventh grades.

College Search Function

If you check "yes" on the Student Search Service section on the PSAT to allow colleges to see information about your student, you'll be well on your way to starting your college search. This is a good thing, because colleges will start marketing to your student. You can find out about great colleges this way - perfect fit colleges you otherwise may not have considered. Yours could be the student they want! They may be looking for a homeschooled student in Oregon who wants to be a doctor, or may be willing to take *any* student from North Dakota, merely to get another state represented at their school. The Student Search can tell you which colleges want *your* child. By the end of junior year, you should know where your child wants to apply, and it can help to request that interested colleges mail you information.

Make sure your student fills out the student information section as well. They will be asked questions about what classes they have taken in high school. Since homeschoolers rarely talk about that sort of thing, sometimes kids don't have a clue what courses they have taken, or what grades moms intend to give them.

Taking the PSAT for Profit!

The second part of the name of this test is NMSQT. Although people rarely refer to the test this way, it indicates that the test is "for profit." This acronym stands for National Merit Scholarship Qualifying Test. If you have heard of a student becoming a "National Merit Scholar" or "National Merit Commended Student," they took *this* test. It's national because everyone can take it, even homeschoolers. It measures academic merit, meaning that a good score and quality academics will get your child considered for the scholarship.

Students who earn the National Merit Scholarship are awarded financial aid for college in the amount of $2500 per year or more. It's a qualifying test because it's the beginning of the scholarship process; first your child takes the test and then there are other hoops to jump through. The test can lead to other scholarships.

Only juniors can take the test for profit. Although younger students can take the test, only juniors' scores count for the NMSQT function of the test. Otherwise, the test is simply for fun. The sophomore year test does *not* count toward the National Merit Scholarship.

Since the PSAT is a practice test for the SAT, it can be for profit even if your child doesn't win the scholarship. College financial aid is often tied to SAT scores and anything you do to raise the score can save you thousands of dollars. Raising your child's score can be as easy as practice, practice, practice. Taking the PSAT is the best way to mimic the SAT test experience. It has the same environment, the same kids, the same noises, sights, and smells as the real test. Using it as a practice test can save you money on college.

Register for the Test

Schools sometimes register kids in June, before classes end for the summer. Other schools register for the test during the first week of school. It's easy to access as a homeschooler, but you must be mindful of the registration deadline, as it is early in the school year. On the College Board web page for homeschooled students, you can search for a school offering the test.

Find a school first, but then call them right away. The test is only offered once each year, and it's easy to miss if you put off the call. The College Board says:

"If you are a home-schooled student, contact a principal or counselor at a local public or independent high school to make arrangements to take the PSAT/NMSQT at their school. Be sure to do so well in advance of the mid-October test dates, preferably during the previous June."

Study for the Test?

I rarely suggest that your child study for the PSAT. Instead, I like to think of taking it as the starting point for studying for the SAT. But for some students, it makes sense to study for this test. If your child has a good chance of earning the National Merit Scholarship, for example, then studying for the PSAT might be that little extra they need. For an anxious student, practice may help them feel comfortable with the "process" of testing.

If you want your child to study for the test, there are options. If you register with www.Petersons.com, you can get one free online sample test. You can also find PSAT test prep books on Amazon such as *Workout for the New PSAT/NMSQT*. When you register for the test, you will also receive one free official student guide to the PSAT, which includes a sample test. Make sure you read the guide, because it offers a lot of helpful information.

Two Weeks to the PSAT: One Simple Step a Day to Prepare for the PSAT

Since I don't suggest cramming for the test, or quizzing kids until they cry, let me make a few suggestions to make their lives *more* pleasant. When there are only two weeks until the PSAT, I want you and your child to be relaxed and ready!

1. Make Sure Your Child Has Photo ID

The PSAT can lead to a National Merit Scholarship - which means a lot of money. They need to make sure that each student is who they say they are. Your child will need some identification with a picture! Does your child have photo ID yet? You can use a driver's license or state identification card. Some homeschool families create their own "school photo ID" to use for the test. This photo ID will be useful for other purposes, including all the tests your child may take in high school, so if they don't have a driver's permit or license, it may be worth it to get a state-issued ID. Get one today, so your child is ready to go. On test day, be sure to bring photo identification and introduce your child to the staff on duty.

2. Adjust Sleep Cycles

It's so important to wake up refreshed for the test! The PSAT occurs early in the morning on a Wednesday (or Saturday), and it's not done at the kitchen table, so there is a commute involved. Part of getting a good score means showing up for the test well rested. Not everyone can wake up bright-eyed and bushy-tailed at 6:00 am to take a long test. Give your child the best chance of being conscious by sliding their bedtime over the next few weeks, so they are used to getting up early and can be as rested as possible. This is probably the most challenging tip! But try anyway, and see what you can do. Good luck with that ...

3. Review Your Transcript

During the test, your child will need to fill out information about their school, so explain your homeschool to your child before they take it. The pre-test student information section asks for the student's grade average and estimated exit date for high school. In other words, before the test even begins, the questions are about the student's performance at school. That can be difficult for a homeschool child, who has never seen a report card, and perhaps doesn't know that "social studies" means "history class." It can cause anxiety when a child feels like they have some questions answered incorrectly, before the test even begins! Prepare your child for these questions by showing them their high school transcript and discussing it before the test. Show them the classes they have taken, and explain the grades you have given. If you need help, you can create a quick transcript with the Total Transcript Solution on The HomeScholar website. It has a free bonus called "Emergency Transcript

Help" if you need to get yours done quickly.

4. Review the Student Guide

Your child will need to fill in bubbles to enter their personal information before the test begins. When kids are told not to give strangers their information, they may not know what to do in this situation. They need to know it is ok for them to provide their full name and address. They also need to include their grade level and classes they have taken, and there are questions about their plans for college and college major. Plan now to help students accurately "grid-in" their information on an answer sheet by practicing filling in bubbles. Prepare them for these questions. Otherwise, your child may feel confused or anxious, and that can make them upset before the test even begins.

When you registered, you received one PSAT practice test. Parents should read all the information in this package, and share important information. Do you want your child to give their social security number? I do not recommend this. They will request your email, so discuss whether your child should provide it. They also offer a "Student Search Service" and I think participation in it is a good idea so you get information from colleges that may want your student.

5. Take One Practice Test

When you registered, you received one PSAT practice test. Use it to your advantage! By taking the practice test, your child will begin to understand the format of the test. They will understand how to "grid in" answers. They will understand that each section is timed, and they will have the opportunity to understand the directions for each section. Don't send your child in completely unprepared. Taking the sample test in the comfort of your own home can help them understand what the test will be like, and reduce the fear of the unknown.

6. Provide a Healthy Snack

This test is not like a 50-minute math test. It's very long, with many sections. It's important to keep your child thinking clearly during the test. One big key is providing nutrition during the test; you aren't going to be there to feed your little hobbit "second breakfast" as they may normally enjoy at home. Plan for mid-morning snack by bringing a healthy treat and water. You don't want them bouncing off the wall, you want them to be fed, hydrated, and ready to perform at their peak. Juices can spike blood sugar much like candy, and a lot of research shows that hydration can improve brain function, so I suggest bringing bottled water and a protein bar they enjoy.

7. Bring Four Sharpened Pencils

The test must be completed with a "Number 2" pencil. The nightmare scenario is using a broken pencil during the test, while the timer is going. This test waits for no student! It can reduce anxiety to have a backup pencil easily accessible. The test is hours long, though, so these pencils will get used a lot. It's not as though your child can get up in the middle of the test to find a pencil sharpener. For this reason, I suggest taking multiple sharpened pencils, plus a manual pencil sharpener. Talk to your child about putting their spare pencils on the desk when they first sit down, so they are ready when needed. For techie students, make sure they are used to a pencil, and know how to use a manual pencil sharpener. For overly-kind and considerate homeschoolers, sending them with multiple pencils can allow them to share a sharp pencil with a neighbor if asked, while not putting themselves at a disadvantage because they shared.

8. No Candy During Tests

Candy is a great reward for a job well done, but don't give your child candy to take to the test! A sudden jolt of sugar can increase energy levels, but the problem is that it's temporary. The sugar rush will only last a short time, and then when the body compensates for all the sugar, your child is left with a candy crash, and low blood sugar levels. Ultimately, giving your child sugar for the test may help them perform well for the first half hour, but after that, they will perform much worse. It's tempting as a parent to try to help them by providing candy. Don't do it! It can reduce their test score. Save it until after the test.

9. Get Familiar with the Calculator

Using calculators for high school math is important, so they can quickly calculate facts and still have enough time for complicated equations. If you haven't started allowing calculators, now is the time. It's still important to use mental math to estimate an answer first, to be sure the calculator answer is accurate. Part of scoring well is answering questions quickly, so a calculator can make a huge difference. You need the right calculator, though - one that is simple enough to use, and familiar enough so they can use it quickly. Bring a calculator your child knows how to use and is the most comfortable with. Now is no time for them to be fiddling around with a new gadget, or looking for the plus sign in the wrong place. Calculators on electronic devices are not allowed. By the way, do your children know that turning off electronic devices means "off" not "mute"?

10. Identify Pick-up Location

Homeschoolers don't spend their days in a public school, and may never have stepped foot into the test location before. A new environment can be stressful for a child, and you can make it easier by dropping them off at the correct room and picking them up promptly. As you walk into the test venue, choose a pick up location. Show them exactly where they will be when the test has ended and be ready to pick them up on time. You may want to bring a book to read while you are waiting for your child. Although the test sections are timed, the breaks between sections can make the test longer, so you may need to wait. Don't worry! If they seem like they are late coming out of the test, it means they were given enough time between sections to clear their mind. It's not a bad thing! But in case they are earlier than expected, you will want to be ready to pick them up.

11. Find Your State Homeschool Code

Each school has a code number and all test results with that code number are sent to the school. Homeschoolers should use the homeschool code and the test results will be sent directly to your home, because you are the school. When the student fills out the personal information on their answer sheet, they enter their state's homeschool code instead of a school code. You can find the homeschool code for every test, including the PSAT, in my blog post, "Homeschool Codes for Tests." The PSAT Homeschool Code will vary by state because the National Merit Scholarship is determined on a state-by-state basis. Homeschoolers are compared with other students within their state, not compared against the nation. Here is the good news – the test proctors will know the homeschool code!

Don't panic if you forget to write it down, because generally someone in charge can tell you what it is, or will know how to find the information. The College Board website provides a list of state homeschool codes.

12. Eat a Breakfast with Protein

Have I mentioned that the PSAT is a long test? The test itself is only a couple of hours, but from the time you leave home until you pick up your child can be a long time! It takes a long time for the test administrator to coordinate a test with so many children and get everyone settled. Then the students have to fill out the personal information, which also takes a while, and the test hasn't even begun yet! Include the time allowed for breaks and it adds up to a long test. It is a long time for a child to be expected to perform well, and a nutritious breakfast is critical. Once, when I picked up my child from a test, one young woman walked out looking very pale. She was explaining to another girl that she had forgotten to eat breakfast that morning - and it was well past noon! Give your child a good breakfast they like, that includes protein, so they will stay full and satisfied for a long time, and are able to think their best, all the way through until the end of the test.

13. Locate the Bathroom

I can't over-state the importance of this one! By far the most important tip for the day is to locate the bathroom. The homeschool kids at the test may have no idea where the bathroom is, how long it takes to walk there, or how to find their way back to the test afterward. Now is no time to act cool - now is the time to locate that bathroom! I know one young person who took the test and skipped the bathroom break, because they were unsure where it was located. Later, because the bathroom was urgently needed, part of a section was left completely blank while the bathroom was located mid-test. Failing to locate the bathroom before the PSAT can cost points on the test.

14. This is a Practice Test

The PSAT is a practice SAT test, not a test that determines your child's future. Unless your child is a junior, and regularly scores above the 95th percentile, this test will be simply for practice. It's best to take a practice test in a real-life situation. Sure, practicing at home and timing each section can give your child some practice, but nothing can prepare your child for taking a college admission test the way a real test can! Sitting with so many other people, with all the distractions, can be a challenge! Your child may experience the ambiance of sneezing, swearing, tattooed, pierced, and strangely dressed teenagers. When your child is taking the PSAT, only part of preparation is about the test itself, the rest is preparation for the test environment. No matter how your child performs on the test, this is only practice. It's practice for the SAT test environment, and that is irreplaceable. Why do colleges care how your child does on a fill-in-the-bubble test with 500 other people? Because at many large universities, it's what every test is like. Understanding the test environment is part of being prepared for college. This test isn't only practice for the SAT, it's also practice for college.

15. Celebrate Success

Time to celebrate! When your child is done the test, think of a way to mark the occasion with fun. Plan a special meal or birthday-like surprise. Crafty super-moms might make a "You did it!" cake or a pizza cookie spelling out "I survived the PSAT." Try to think of a way to make this whole experience blend into a positive memory for your child. The main purpose is to practice for college admission tests they need to take in the future. Do what you can to make this a pleasant memory, so they won't be overwhelmingly nervous or upset before the next test. At this point, the definition of success is that your sweet child has done it - completed the test - and lived to tell the tale. It's a rite of passage and a symbol of adulthood. It deserves a pat on the back!

For PSAT printable tips, check out the article, "2 Weeks to the PSAT" on The HomeScholar website. Place one tip on the breakfast plate each morning!

National Merit Scholarship

Have you seen billboards and newspaper articles announcing that a student is a National Merit Scholar? Did you know that these students entered the competition by taking the PSAT? The National Merit Scholarship is the best-known high school scholarship in the nation, and the only way to win is to start with the PSAT test. Therefore, the single most important thing you can do to win this scholarship is to make sure your children take the PSAT in October of 11th grade.

Students are invited to participate in the competition based on their Selection Index from the PSAT, compared to other students within each state. The Selection Index is used to compare high school juniors within each state. Because each state is different, it's impossible to predict exactly how your child will compare. However, if your student's scores are above the 98th percentile on the PSAT, there is a possibility they may qualify for the National Merit Scholarship.

Monetary Amount Varies

The National Merit Scholarship is a non-renewable, one-time award of up to $2500. Not everyone gets the whole prize amount, and some will get far less. When you compare the award to the cost of colleges, it doesn't seem like much. But the National Merit Scholarship can be a stepping-stone to other scholarships.

Corporate-sponsored Merit Scholarship awards can provide additional money for some students. College-sponsored Merit Scholarship awards usually provide the most money. Colleges love to publicize how many National Merit Scholars they have on campus. College-sponsored merit scholarships can be very large, even full scholarships. Some colleges will only give their largest monetary award to a student who names the college as their first choice university, and will provide lesser scholarships to other National Merit Scholars. On the other end of the spectrum are colleges that provide special scholarships to any National Merit participants, not only the winners, including commended students and semi-finalists.

National Merit Scholarship Process

The National Merit Scholarship competition is a long, drawn-out process, lasting over a year. PSAT scores are available a month or two after the child takes the test. The competition is based on the Selection Index score of high school juniors. The Selection Index is the sum of all three sections of the test: reading, writing, and math. Although you can clearly see the Selection Index on the PSAT score report, you can't tell how your student did in comparison to the other students across your state, so you won't immediately know whether they will advance in the scholarship competition. Scholarship participants are chosen by state, so students are only compared to other high school juniors

Although you receive PSAT test scores during junior year, it's not until the following August or September of senior year that Commended Students are notified and for them the competition has ended. Later, some students will be notified they are semi-finalists, and for them the competition continues. Semi-finalists must complete a detailed scholarship application demonstrating the academic rigor of their education. They must take the SAT test, which will confirm the validity of their PSAT performance, and their SAT score must be reported to the National Merit Corporation. Homeschoolers have become National Merit Scholars, and parents must play the role of school administrator, providing documentation of a rigorous education through well-documented record keeping.

Fine print details abound. The PSAT only counts toward the National Merit Scholarship Competition during the third year of a four-year high school, which is usually junior year. However, the administrators do understand that bright and gifted kids sometimes graduate early.

Planning for Success

If your child tends to score in the 90th percentile or higher on standardized tests, there is the possibility of winning these awards. There are also things you can do to increase your child's chances of winning. Have your child take the PSAT in 10th grade for practice, so they are comfortable with the test-taking environment. During 10th grade, have your children study for the PSAT regularly, teaching the skills of reading, writing, and math in the context of test preparation. Familiarity with the test can increase test scores. Plan to complete geometry before sophomore year or earlier, if possible, to maximize the score on the math section. Carefully notice the deadlines at your testing site to register for the PSAT, so you don't miss it. Make sure your homeschool records and course descriptions are up to date, so you can demonstrate academic rigor if your child advances to the semi-finalist stage.

The complete process of winning a National Merit Scholarship can be a bit complicated, and the information here can only provide an overview. If you are notified that your child is a semi-finalist, immediately spend time doing research. For general information on the PSAT, go to www.collegeboard.com. For detailed information on the PSAT, search www.professionals.collegeboard.com and read the PSAT/NMSQT Supervisor's Manual. For general information on the National Merit Scholarship, go to their website, www.nationalmerit.org and read their information about entering the competitions.

National Merit Scholarship Planning Timeline

10th grade

October 10th grade – take the PSAT for fun and practice

11th grade

May - September 11th grade – register for the PSAT

October 11th grade – take the PSAT for the National Merit Scholarship

December 11th grade – scores available

Spring 11th grade – take the SAT

12th grade

September 12th grade – commended and Semi-Finalists are notified

October 12th grade – parents are "the school" and must complete the application

December 12th grade – SAT scores must be sent to National Merit Corporation

February 12th grade – finalists notified

March 12th grade – National Merit Scholarship

April 12th grade - Corporate-sponsored scholarships awarded

May 12th grade – National Merit Scholars are notified

Summer after 12th grade – scholarship awards are announced to the media

Missed the PSAT?

Sometimes in her heart of hearts, a mom will know that her child could qualify for the National Merit Scholarship. If this describes you, what do you do when your child misses the PSAT? There is a way to apply for the National Merit Scholarship even if your child has missed the test.

If a Student Misses the PSAT/NMSQT

A student who does not take the PSAT/NMSQT because of illness, an emergency, or other extenuating circumstance, but meets all other requirements for NMSC program participation, may still be able to enter the competition. The student or a school official must write to NMSC as soon as possible after PSAT/NMSQT administration to request information about procedures for entry to the NMSC competition by alternate testing. The earlier NMSC receives the written request, the greater the student's opportunities for meeting alternate entry requirements. To be considered, a request must be postmarked no later than March 1st following the PSAT/NMSQT administration that was missed. NMSC will provide alternate entry materials, including an entry form that requires the signature of a school official.

This can only work in cases of serious emergency, though. Simply missing the test is not enough to enter the competition. If you plan to request an alternate entry this way, follow their directions carefully, and be sure to be exceptionally clear and concise. Good luck!

The PSAT 10

The PSAT 10 is the exact same test as the PSAT/NMSQT. Why is there a PSAT 10 test? For more practice, the PSAT 10 is offered in February or March of tenth grade only (the "10" part of the test). Like the PSAT, your child will receive score reports, which can help direct further study on Khan Academy and help steer your child toward appropriate AP tests if you desire.

Since students already take the PSAT twice, I don't believe it's necessary to add a third time in the form of the PSAT 10. However, if you believe your child needs more practice or would like more practice, then do what's best for your child.

Chapter 3

ACT

The ACT is a standardized test that will meet any state test assessment requirements. It covers reading, writing, math, and science. Science is not tested on the SAT, which is why some colleges accept the ACT test, since they don't need to request a separate science subject test. The ACT offers an optional writing section, scored on a scale of one to six. A score of one means the student can't put two words together, and a six means their writing is excellent.

A perfect overall score on the ACT is 36, with the average score around 20, although this varies by state. A score over 21 is good, and over 24 is great.

Some colleges give great scholarships for scores over 24.

Except for the optional essay, the ACT consists of all multiple-choice questions. Like the SAT, there is no penalty for guessing. Some statistics show that girls score better on the ACT, which might be something to keep in mind. Currently, the cost of the ACT is $39.50 without the essay section and $56.50 with the essay.

How Do You Decide?

When it comes to college admissions, schools all over the country seem to have their own preferences for either the SAT or the ACT. While schools on the coasts most often prefer the SAT, those in the middle of the country seem to prefer the ACT. Many colleges accept both. In order to determine which test your child should take, check the colleges your child is interested in for their specific preferences.

One-third of students tend to do better on the SAT, one-third do better on the

ACT, and one-third show no difference in scores between tests. If you have the option of submitting either test to your college-of-choice, have your child take a sample SAT and ACT test at home. Try both tests, without pressure, and see which test makes your child look like a genius. Then decide which test to take for college admission.

You can get sample tests online at www.collegeboard.com and www.act.org. You can also go to the library and check out an SAT and ACT book, and take the sample tests included. The librarian may be willing to make copies of the tests for you. Each test is about three hours long, which is a total pain, but worth it!

One of my clients' daughters earned a full scholarship *plus* room and board, *plus* books and expenses, *plus* a $600 stipend to attend her first choice college. The mom said she was thankful for my help, so I asked her about my most helpful recommendation. She credited my advice on sampling both tests. She said she would *never* have guessed that her daughter would do better on the

ACT, and it didn't make sense to her, but she pre-tested her daughter, and registered her for the ACT instead.

Even if your child tests well in general, most kids do worse on one of the tests, so it can still save you money. You don't know unless you try. Once you have decided which test makes your child look like a genius, help them study for that test. If the ACT is the right test for your child, The Princeton Review offers materials to help study for it. *Cracking the ACT with 6 Practice Tests* is a good book for studying.

PLAN

This is a pre-ACT test, which is meant to be taken in tenth grade. It is for practice and it's used to predict the ACT test score. It will meet any state standardized test assessment requirement and is often tied to scholarships.

Chapter 4

Subject Tests

AP - SAT - CLEP – Making Sense of the Acronym Avalanche

There are many different high school subject tests to choose from. Perhaps you have already heard about the AP Test or AP classes from your homeschool group. Maybe you have heard about required SAT Subject Tests, or wondered about CLEP tests after hearing them mentioned at a convention seminar. Let me explain them all, plain and simple in one quick overview, to get you started in the right direction.

Who – College Bound High School Students

College bound students, especially those destined for selective schools, should consider taking subject tests. Subject tests can be helpful because they are a common measurement of a student's understanding of the material.

Many colleges understand these tests, and some require them for admission. Most colleges require either the SAT or ACT test as outside documentation, but some want more in the form of subject tests. Not all require SAT Subject tests. Fewer still require AP Exams. No colleges *require* CLEP tests, but some *accept* them, to strengthen the college application.

What – SAT Subject Test, AP Test, CLEP Test

- **SAT Subject Tests** are one-hour long, multiple-choice tests that measure a high school amount of learning in a specific subject. SAT Subject Tests are quick, don't require specialized learning, and are intended to demonstrate general high school knowledge.

- **AP Tests** are three hours long, most include essays, and they measure a college amount of knowledge. AP Tests assume that a student has taken rigorous AP classes approved by the College Board. Special AP classes are not required, however. Anyone can take an AP test, even if they have not taken an AP course.
- **CLEP Exams** are computer-based multiple-choice exams offered year round that can provide college credit. CLEP exams are college level tests that assume a student has learned naturally through reading, visiting museums, reading the paper, and engaging in hands-on learning. These exams are often a great fit for homeschoolers because they don't assume everything was learned in a classroom setting.

Where – Tests Given at Schools

Public and private high schools usually host subject tests. The SAT Subject Tests are offered multiple times a year, often at the same location as the SAT or ACT exams. The AP Exams are also offered at schools in May when AP classes are over. CLEP exams are unusual, because people who are not in public high school typically take them. They are given at computer test centers at colleges, technical schools, or community colleges.

When – After Studying Each Subject

Most students take subject tests in their sophomore and junior year so their results are ready to present to colleges with their applications in senior year. Some students take them earlier. In most cases, you should give tests immediately after your child has completed study of the subject, so the information is still fresh. In other words, have your child take the chemistry exam right after they finish their chemistry class.

Why – Demonstrate Knowledge of Specific Subjects

Subject tests are useful to prove your child has learned a subject thoroughly. In an objective, measurable way, these tests demonstrate achievement in one subject at a time. The SAT or ACT test can demonstrate a general understanding of reading, writing, and math, but they aren't specific. It can be helpful to take a subject test in each broad subject category: math, English, history, science, and foreign language. If a college wants two subject tests, have your child take the two tests in which they will perform best, in the subjects they enjoy most.

How – Ensure Passing Scores

Register for each test months in advance, so you don't miss the deadline, but don't let your student take a test unprepared. Have your child take a sample test at home, to make sure they know the material. Then help them study for the test using study guides at home, filling in any gaps in the information. Sit your child down to take full-length, timed sample tests to be sure the student can succeed. Then have them take the real test at a testing location.

The bottom line is, never let your child take a test if you believe they will not pass. It can hurt their future testing ability, and cause problems with your child's self-perception. Pre-test at home to make sure your child is comfortable with the material and the test format. Only let them take a real test once you are confident they can pass it. If you aren't certain your child will earn an acceptable score, don't have scores sent to colleges until after you have seen the results.

Finding the Details You Need to Succeed

Now that you know the basics about the tests, there are other considerations, such as stress. It's unusual for a child to go to college classes or take a college test without feeling some stress. A bit of stress can be helpful, so children can learn to deal with stressful test situations. On the other hand, you don't want to build up anxiety in your child needlessly until they develop a phobia of tests. You don't want to ask them to take a test they aren't comfortable with.

When I worked as a nurse, we used the "five rights" of medication administration to avoid errors: the right patient, the right drug, the right dose, the right route, and the right time. Using this same strategy, here are the "five rights" of high school subject test success.

The Five "Rights" of High School Subject Tests

1. The Right Test – Decide Which Tests are Best

Choose the best test for your child. If your child is taking advanced classes and wants to attend a selective college, an AP test may be best. Independent learners with advanced knowledge might do best on a CLEP test. If your child is working at grade level, but not taking honors classes, then perhaps SAT

Subject Tests are best. If you aren't sure what level your child is in a subject, or if you are unschooling, then SAT Subject Tests might be helpful.

2. The Right College - Know What Your College Wants

Colleges may require subject tests. Some colleges require up to five or more SAT Subject Tests from all applicants (not only homeschoolers). It can help to know which tests your chosen colleges might require ahead of time, and then try to exceed their expectations for college admission and scholarship success. You can meet or exceed their expectations by taking tests that make your student look most desirable. Do an online search for the names of your college choices plus "admission requirements." Remember that college policies change over time, so contact the college directly, before senior year, to find out any additional, updated information.

3. The Right Day – Watch the Calendar

Once you have decided which tests you want your child to take, keep track of test dates. Each year, add important dates to your calendar or planner, such as registration deadlines, the date of each test, and dates you will receive results. Include the location and test code you will need on test day on your calendar. You can find these codes in my article, "Homeschool Codes for Tests" on The HomeScholar website. Send the test results to each college during senior year, if you haven't already.

4. The Right Preparation – Study for Tests

There are four steps for studying:

- First, your child has to learn the subject, using curriculum and resources that match their learning style.
- While the subject is still fresh in their mind, pick up a study guide for the test, to prepare your child

for the exact questions they will encounter.

- Next, you need to identify the information they haven't learned yet - topics that might be on the test but weren't in the curriculum. Take the time to fill any gaps.
- Finally, have your child take sample tests repeatedly, to practice timing, speed, filling in bubbles, and writing essays. This will help them earn the maximum scores. If sample test scores aren't acceptable, consider other tests or options.

Study is important, but there are many things beyond test preparation you can do to improve your child's test score. Sleep, nutrition, and hydration are remarkably important!

A few weeks in advance of each test, slide your child's sleep schedule back so they will be ready to work the morning of the test. On test day, make sure they have a good breakfast. They should also bring a snack and water for breaks. Be sure to check the test location in advance, so you know exactly where it is, and can ensure your child arrives rested and unhurried. Don't forget to bring ID for the test, because they are careful to prevent cheating.

5. The Right Resources – Find Information for Each Test

Choosing a study guide and resources can be a challenge. Read the reviews first, because study guides change frequently. The resources below will help you decide on the right test, check out the format, and locate independent study guides you can use at home.

SAT Subject Tests

Research SAT Subject Tests: collegereadiness.collegeboard.org/sat-subject-tests

Take Sample SAT Subject Tests: *The Official Study Guide for All SAT Subject Tests*

Study Guides for SAT Subject Tests: Princeton Review Books

AP Tests

Research AP Subject Tests: apstudent.collegeboard.org/home

Take Sample AP Subject Tests: apstudent.collegeboard.org/takingtheexam/preparing-for-exams

Study Guides for AP Subject Tests: Princeton Review Books

CLEP Exams

Research CLEP Exams: clep.collegeboard.org/started

Take Sample CLEP Exams: *CLEP Official Study Guide for all 33 Exams*

Study Guides for CLEP Exams: CLEP Study Guides by REA

If you need additional help, look to the test prep companies specifically geared to the test you need, such as Kaplan and The Princeton Review. You can also hire a tutor. While a general tutor may be helpful for general subjects and test-taking strategies, specific tests may require targeted preparation. Look for tutors and classes with specific expertise.

Summary for Overwhelmed Parents

How Do You Decide?

I know that some parents are completely in over their head, near-tears right now, and possibly panic-stricken. Don't stop homeschooling merely because all these different subject tests exist! You only *need* to think about the tests your college requires. Here's a simple summary on how to choose.

Reasons for Choosing SAT Subject Tests

1. Some colleges require them.

2. *Your* chosen college requires them, as you found out during a college search

3. You are unsure what to put on the transcript, and these tests indicate knowledge of the subject

Reasons for choosing AP

1. Confidence that your child will have every test that might be required

2. Reduce cost of college by earning college credit for work done in high school

3. Success with college studies, because AP study mimics college work

Reasons for choosing CLEP

1. Earn a college degree by taking many exams that are accredited by a college

2. Reduce the cost of college by taking a few exams for college credit

3. Validate learning in specific subjects, so colleges know the sum of your child's knowledge

Of course, the difficulty is knowing which colleges your child may want to attend. If you can't determine this in advance, let me give you a one-size-fits-most suggestion. Plan to have your child take five SAT Subject Tests, one during sophomore year, and two each during junior and senior year. This is usually the number required by colleges that want to see subject tests.

Once your child finishes the tests, you have the option of including test scores on your homeschool transcript. It's optional. If the scores make your child look smarter (good scores), then include them on the transcript. If the scores do not make your child look smarter (bad scores), then leave them off the transcript.

While you do need to meet college admission requirements, if these tests aren't right for your child, there are other ways to earn outside documentation. Dual enrollment, letters of recommendation, comprehensive homeschool records, excellent application essays, and a work resume can also increase your child's chances of earning college admission and scholarships. Learn more about this in my article, "Outside Documentation" at The HomeScholar website.

Remember, know your child and trust yourself. As always, do what's best for your child.

Chapter 5

CLEP and DSST

If your student is looking for ways to earn college credit while still in high school, CLEP and DSST college level tests are great resources. Thousands of colleges accept credit by examination, so this is a great way to fast track or cut time (and money) off a college degree.

CLEP

CLEP stands for College Level Examination Program. CLEP tests are subject tests that measure one subject at a time, with about 33 subjects available. Because it's a subject test, it does not meet your annual assessment requirement. Many colleges accept these tests and give credit for them, but check with the individual colleges where your child is interested in applying first.

CLEP test scores range from 20-80; a passing score is anything above 50 for most tests. Each college will decide what score is required to award college credit. Foreign languages may have a higher score requirement, such as a 60 or 65 in order to earn college credit.

One of the unusual things about the CLEP is that it is computer-based. Other subject tests use paper and pencil at a local high school. CLEP tests usually take place in computer labs at a university, vocational college, or community college. Military bases also offer CLEP tests. The College Board lists testing centers located close to you. Because colleges host these tests, they are typically available year-round. Since the test is completed on a computer, your child's score will be immediately available after they finish the test.

The College Board accumulates CLEP test scores and sends them to any colleges you designate in transcript form. The transcript looks identical to a community college or university transcript, so it's official looking and provides solid outside documentation to affirm your homeschool coursework.

Many public school families have not heard about CLEP because high schools don't offer the tests, but CLEP tests have been around for a long time. Historically, they were offered to adults and college students. Colleges are used to seeing CLEP tests, as college students take them all the time. Adults can take CLEP tests to satisfy undergraduate requirements and get into college right away.

In order to prepare for the CLEP test, I suggest you use the *CLEP Official Study Guide*. There is a new one available every year, but they don't change a lot over time, so if you use one that's three or four years old, it probably hasn't changed. The study guide includes one assessment test for each available subject, which you should use to assess your student. It's important to make sure your student will do well on the test before they take it, so assessing their readiness is critical.

DSST

DSST used to be called Dante's. It is also a credit by exam program, and tests one subject at a time. DSST measures information your child has learned before, and it's usually heavy on business and social sciences. There are 38 subjects offered by DSST. Over 2,000 colleges and universities recognize the program and award college credit for passing scores. Colleges, universities, and corporations throughout the United States and in other countries around the world administer tests year-round.

This is a much newer test program that originated in the U.S. military. Most colleges have a policy on DSST tests. Check a college's "credit by examination" section to determine whether they accept these credits or not. Unlike CLEP, the College Board does not

administer this test. For more information,
visit www.GetCollegeCredit.com.

Lee Binz, The HomeScholar

Chapter 6

Placement Tests

If your student is planning to enroll in a community college course, it is likely that the college will require them to take a placement test. A placement test helps the college evaluate incoming students' skill levels in reading, writing, math, and English as a Second Language. It helps the college determine appropriate courses the student should be placed in according to their abilities, and connects them to the resources the college provides for academic success.

Sometimes a college will only require non-English speakers to take a placement test, not people who speak English as their first language. This is a valuable test to take prior to enrollment, because you wouldn't want your student to be placed in a course that is too difficult for them, or a course in which they would be completely bored!

The test is important for accurate college level placement. If your student gets an A on the math section, they can take Pre-Calculus at the college; if they get a passing grade on reading and writing, they can take English 101. If they don't pass the English section of the test, they will need to take a remedial English class at the college before taking more advanced English classes.

The math portion of a placement test is usually broken down into sections. For instance, the student might pass pre-algebra, algebra, and college level algebra, but not trigonometry. This type of test can be helpful for families who have unschooled, and who don't know what their children have picked up naturally in math. A placement test can help you know that your student has passed pre-algebra and algebra level work, which you can then put on their transcript, since they know the material.

In a college catalog, classes may state, "This class is open to students who have passed the placement test with a score over 65." This is how they weed out those who don't have the skills needed in order to succeed in the class. A placement test can be taken more than once, so if your child passed the reading and writing, but did not pass the math, they can go back and take the math section again.

ACCUPLACER

The ACCUPLACER test is a specific placement test for community college admission. Offered by the College Board, this test covers reading, writing, math, and English as a Second Language. It does include a written essay, which can help you figure out which English class is appropriate for your child.

On average, 40% of students who have been admitted into a university need some remedial help in reading, writing, and/or math. As a result, colleges are careful to do a placement test before students register for classes.

To help your child succeed in college, include a math class when they are a senior in high school. It's also a good idea to prepare them emotionally for the possibility of an assessment test in reading, writing, and math before they register for classes. Be prepared!

Chapter 7

Testing on the Bell-Shaped Curve

In the fictional town of Lake Wobegon, the children are all above average. Every parent would like to think their own children are above average, but scientifically, we know that children are all located somewhere within the bell-shaped curve of academic performance. Too often, parents judge their own or others' children based on relative position along the curve. They tend to ignore the uniqueness and individuality that makes life more meaningful. Homeschoolers are no exception. Let me explain what the bell-shaped curve looks like from different perspectives, so you can see how it may affect your day-to-day life and social interactions.

On the Left

On the left of the bell-shaped curve are children who test below grade level. They may even be academically behind. Homeschooling works, because it can improve their academic performance level, even allowing children to achieve grade level in their most challenging subjects. These children thrive at home, without teachers labeling them or children teasing them. Parents can use a learning style that works for their child, and keep the repetitive work to the minimum their child needs in order to practice and learn. These children can pursue learning without having to lean on their weakest ability. If reading is a challenge, your child can learn through listening, if writing is difficult your child can answer questions orally. Without being slowed down by their unique learning challenges, children can progress through grade level and beyond.

The problem is that some children will not excel academically, and may never quite make it to the 50th percentile, even with great struggle. For them, achieving the 50th percentile can represent a huge success that few parents with average or above average children would understand. While they are celebrating success beyond their wildest dreams, their friends may still offer advice and make suggestions, assuming something is wrong without recognizing how much is going right.

Without seeing how it might hurt the parent who is doing incredibly well with their outside-of-average child, thoughtless comments do damage, even when well intended. The mother or father may internalize negative messages and begin to think they are less than capable or not doing enough. Remember to listen before jumping to conclusions. A parent is a successful homeschooler if their child is performing to the best of their ability.

On the Right

On the right of the bell-shaped curve are children who test above grade level. They may be engaged in advanced courses as well. Some of these bright or profoundly gifted children are also socially awkward or bookish. Others might be charmers, kids who are prom-king or queen material and seem like the proverbial five-tool players in baseball. Homeschooling works because these children can learn at their own accelerated pace, with their parents carefully choosing curriculum to balance their academic needs and social maturity. Parents can find a curriculum for anything, no matter how advanced, so these kids can learn independently and become self-motivated, self-educated students of advanced topics.

Outsiders want to label these children, too. People tend to think that all gifted children are either awkward or charismatic over-achievers. These children have innate gifts that can't be changed. Friends don't understand what the parent of a gifted child may be facing.

They may assume the parents are driving their children too hard to succeed. But, more often, they are desperately trying to keep up. It can feel like being tied to the saddle of a thoroughbred on the racetrack; all you want to do is get off because you aren't a jockey. Like a teenager who is always hungry, these gifted children constantly want more information. It's exhausting and can be incredibly expensive.

Well-meaning friends will try to fix the parents, as if it's their fault the child is smart. They might imply parents are turning their children into nerds by force; they may label the child while suggesting a course of action, "Your child will not be normal unless you ..." Through homeschooling, these parents can meet their children's academic and social needs without requiring excessive busywork. Remember, this parent is also successful; their child is succeeding to the best of their ability.

In the Center

In the center of the bell-shaped curve are parents who get to determine what the words "grade level" and "normal" mean to them. Public school might be a good fit for their children academically, but they choose to homeschool for other reasons. They may homeschool because they feel called to do it. They may worry about socialization, spiritual integrity, bullying, the common core, violence, or lack of discipline in the schools. Their normal children obtain normal test scores in normal test settings, and yet these parents worry their kids are dumb because their scores aren't sky-high. They may be focused on family harmony and home education and not have the time or desire to pick ideological fights.

Parents with kids in the center may choose normal curriculum and may be home educating in an ordinary, every-day, successful way. These parents are judged for their choices as well. Other parents may wonder aloud why they don't push harder so their child can succeed and attend an Ivy League college. Friends may complain that they aren't actively fighting common core. Some of these parents may even be criticized for their religious or political beliefs.

Neighbors don't recognize the hurt they cause. Friends don't understand that homeschooling can still be effective and fulfilling for normal children using grade-level curriculum, even when the parent homeschools for a different reason than they do.

The Center of Kindness

The problem among homeschoolers is that they often see their own successes and think that if other parents homeschooled the same way, they could be successful too. Other parents see their own weaknesses, but do not see the weaknesses of others. Thanks to the perfect pictures and stories on social media, they end up feeling inadequate and incapable of homeschooling. The problem is that homeschoolers think homeschooling will solve everything, from personality traits and learning styles, to salvation and sin nature. In reality, parents and children are individuals, with unique gifts and challenges others can't understand; they make mistakes, as everybody does.

People are less judgmental when they know each other personally. When interacting with your "friends" online, recognize that you know very little about them. When talking with real-life friends, understand that there can be circumstances and a side to the story that you simply can't imagine. Give grace to them. Don't fan the flames of insecurity with judgmental, know-it-all responses.

You have to trust other parents to do what is best for their beloved child. Be nice. Play nice. Be kind. You don't know what the mom next to you is going through. You don't know how her child challenges her, or what constitutes success in her home or homeschool. Ask her, "Are you OK? Tell me about that. It sounds difficult." Share your own struggles. Extend grace. Use kind words.

True kindness is not saying, "Bless your heart!" True kindness is blessing others with genuine words of appreciation and encouragement.

It is time for a kindness revolution in homeschooling. If we must compete, let's strive to be on the same side of that movement, standing together, and building each other up. If we spent our energy on this instead of critiquing and gossiping, we would all end up with happier, healthier children, families and friendships.

Character Qualities Not Measured by Tests

Before or after your child goes into a test, you may want to mention that the test is only an indication of certain academic abilities; it's not a reflection of what is truly important in this world.

Here is a list of some of the character qualities not measured by tests:

•Charity

•Commitment

- Compassion

- Courage

- Creativity

- Critical Thinking

- Curiosity

- Determination

- Endurance

- Enthusiasm

- Faith

- Hope

- Humility

- Humor

- Initiative

- Integrity

- Leadership

- Love

- Love of Learning

- Motivation

- Persistence

- Questioning

- Resilience

- Resourccfulness

- Responsibility

- Self-awareness

- Self-discipline

- Spirituality

- Spontaneity

- Values

- Work Ethic

Tests don't measure everything! Remember to balance your evaluation with other things besides testing!

Resources

Home-Schooled Students and PSAT/NMSQT

- www.collegeboard.org/student/testing/psat/reg/homeschool.html

Homeschooled Students and the SAT

- www.collegeboard.org/parents/tests/meet-tests/21295.html

Learn About the AP

- bigfuture.collegeboard.org/get-in/testing/learn-about-the-ap-program

Learn About the CLEP

- bigfuture.collegeboard.org/get-in/testing/learn-about-the-clep-program

General Information on the SAT

- www.collegeboard.org

Information on ACT

- www.actstudent.org

Study Resources

- The Princeton Review: *Workout for the New PSAT/NMSQT*
- The Princeton Review: *Cracking the ACT with 6 Practice Tests*
- The Princeton Review: *Cracking the New SAT with 4 Practice Tests* (AP, SAT 2 also available)
- The Princeton Review: *500+ Practice Questions for the New SAT*
- The College Board: *CLEP Official Study Guide*
- REA Study Guides: The best test prep for the CLEP exam

- Kaplan: Score-Raising Classics (*Wuthering Heights, Frankenstein*, etc.)

High School Level Tests

PSAT-NMSQT: Evidence-based reading and writing, math.

- One time – October! Register in September at a high school.
- For fun during 10th grade, NMSQT only 11th grade. Sections scored 160-760. www.collegeboard.org

SAT: Evidence-based reading and writing, math

- Essay optional. No penalty for guessing.
- Offered 7 times a year, register online.
- 3 hrs. (plus 50 min. for optional essay). Sections Scored 200-800. www.collegeboard.org

PLAN: Pre-ACT

- 10th grade. Score 1-32. www.act.org

ACT: Reading, writing, math *and* science

- Essay optional, increases cost. No penalty for guessing.
- 6 times yearly, 4 hours. Scored 1-36. www.act.org

SAT Subject Test (SAT II)

- One subject per exam, 1 hour per exam. 6 times a year, register online.
- Scored 200-800 per test. www.collegeboard.org

College Level Tests

AP exams:

- One subject per exam,
- 2-3 hours each.
- Essays and multiple choice required.

- Tests only in May, register by March 15.
- Score 1-5 per test. www.collegeboard.org

CLEP exams:

- One subject per exam.
- 1-1/2 hours per exam.
- Available any day.
- May get college credit.
- Computer based.
- Multiple choice only.
- Scores 20-80, 50-60% to pass. www.collegeboard.org

Placement Tests

- Accuplacer College placement test www.collegeboard.org

Afterword

Who is Lee Binz and What Can She Do for Me?

Number one best-selling homeschool author, Lee Binz is The HomeScholar. Her mission is "helping parents homeschool high school." Lee and her husband, Matt, homeschooled their two boys, Kevin and Alex, from elementary through high school.

Upon graduation, both boys received four-year, full tuition scholarships from their first choice university. This enables Lee to pursue her dream job - helping parents homeschool their children through high school.

On The HomeScholar website, you will find great products for creating homeschool transcripts and comprehensive records to help you amaze and impress colleges.

Find out why Andrew Pudewa, Founder of the Institute for Excellence in Writing says, "Lee Binz knows how to navigate this often confusing and frustrating labyrinth better than anyone."

You can find Lee online at:

www.HomeHighSchoolHelp.com

If this book has been helpful, could you please take a minute to write us a quick review on Amazon?

Thank you!

Testimonials

Eight College Admissions + Scholarships + Pcrks!

"I just wanted to thank you for your help and templates for our daughter's high school transcript and other documentation through the Silver Training membership. Our daughter's high school transcript and other necessary documentation has impressed every (eight in total) college/university she applied to.

She has been accepted to every single one!

They offered her a nice academic scholarship based on her ACT scores, awarded her a nice vocal scholarship, a place in their choir in the fall, an offered her a place on the women's volleyball team in the fall as well. Amazing!"

~ Louisa

"Calming and Practical Advice"

"Just finished watching Homeschool Records that Open Doors! You do a fantastic job on all of the details in this webinar. My stress level has come down so much since finding your site.

You have been so incredibly helpful in ALL of your teachings and webinars; you truly have been given a gift to be able to help so many moms AND dads. Thank you and your family for all of the hard work that has gone into making this site!"

~ Ginger

For more information about my **Comprehensive Record Solution** and **Gold Care Club**, go to:

www.ComprehensiveRecordSolution.com
and
www.GoldCareClub.com

Also From The HomeScholar ...

- The HomeScholar Guide to College Admission and Scholarships: Homeschool Secrets to Getting Ready, Getting In and Getting Paid (Book and Kindle Book)
- Setting the Records Straight - How to Craft Homeschool Transcripts and Course Descriptions for College Admission and Scholarships (Book and Kindle Book)
- TechnoLogic: How to Set Technology Boundaries and Stop the Zombie Apocalypse (Book and Kindle Book)
- Finding the Faith to Homeschool High School: Weekly Reflections for Weary Parents (Book and Kindle Book)

- The HomeScholar Bookshelf (Print Book Collection)
- The Easy Truth About Homeschool Transcripts (Kindle Book)
- Parent Training Classes (Online Training)
- Total Transcript Solution (Online Training, Tools, and Templates)
- Comprehensive Record Solution (Online Training, Tools, and Templates)
- High School Solution (Online Training, Tools and Templates)
- Gold Care Club (Comprehensive Online Support and Training)
- Silver Training Club (Do-it-Yourself Online Training)

The HomeScholar Coffee Break Books Released or Coming Soon on Kindle and Paperback:

- Delight Directed Learning: Guiding Your Homeschooler Toward Passionate Learning
- Creating Transcripts for Your Unique Child: Help Your Homeschool Graduate Stand Out from the Crowd
- Beyond Academics: Preparation for College and for Life

- Planning High School Courses: Charting the Course Toward High School Graduation
- Graduate Your Homeschooler in Style: Make Your Homeschool Graduation Memorable
- Keys to High School Success: Get Your Homeschool High School Started Right!
- Getting the Most Out of Your Homeschool This Summer: Learning just for the Fun of it!
- Finding a College: A Homeschooler's Guide to Finding a Perfect Fit
- College Scholarships for High School Credit: Learn and Earn With This Two-for-One Strategy!
- College Admission Policies Demystified: Understanding Homeschool Requirements for Getting In
- A Higher Calling: Homeschooling High School for Harried Husbands (by Matt Binz, Mr. HomeScholar)
- Gifted Education Strategies for Every Child: Homeschool Secrets for Success
- College Application Essays: A Primer for Parents
- Creating Homeschool Balance: Find Harmony Between Type A and Type Zzz...

- Homeschooling the Holidays: Sanity Saving Strategies and Gift Giving Ideas
- Your Goals this Year: A Year by Year Guide to Homeschooling High School
- Making the Grades: A Grouch-Free Guide to Homeschool Grading
- High School Testing: Knowledge That Saves Money
- Getting the BIG Scholarships: Learn Expert Secrets for Winning College Cash!
- Easy English for Simple Homeschooling: How to Teach, Assess and Document High School English
- Scheduling - The Secret to Homeschool Sanity: Plan You Way Back to Mental Health
- Junior Year is the Key to High School Success: How to Unlock the Gate to Graduation and Beyond
- Upper Echelon Education: How to Gain Admission to Elite Universities
- How to Homeschool College: Save Time, Reduce Stress and Eliminate Debt
- Homeschool Curriculum That's Effective and Fun: Avoid the Crummy Curriculum Hall of Shame!

- Comprehensive Homeschool Records: Put Your Best Foot Forward to Win College Admission and Scholarships
- Options After High School: Steps to Success for College or Career
- How to Homeschool 9th and 10th Grade: Simple Steps for Starting Strong!
- Senior Year Step-by-Step: Simple Instructions for Busy Homeschool Parents
- High School Math The Easy Way: Simple Strategies for Homeschool Parents In Over Their Heads
- How to Homeschool Independently: Do-it-Yourself Strategies to Rekindle the Love of Learning
- Homeschooling Middle School with Powerful Purpose: How to Successfully Navigate 6th through 8th Grade
- Simple Science for Homeschooling High School: Because Teaching Science isn't Rocket Science!

Would you like to be notified when we offer one of our *Coffee Break Books* for FREE during our Kindle promotion days? If so, leave your name and email at the link below and we will send you a reminder.

www.HomeHighSchoolHelp.com/
freekindlebook

Visit my Amazon Author Page!

amazon.com/author/leebinz

Made in the USA
Middletown, DE
16 September 2017